Study and Discussion Guide
to Accompany the Book

GOD OF HOPE

Study and Discussion Guide
to Accompany the Book

GOD OF HOPE

J. DAVIS ILLINGWORTH, JR.

Compiled by Jesse Deloe

BMH Books
www.bmhbooks.com
Winona Lake, IN 46590

Study and Discussion Guide to Accompany the Book God of Hope
Four Men Enter Our World with the Plan

Copyright © J. Davis Illingworth, Jr. 2010
Author: Jesse B. Deloe

ISBN: 978-0-88469-275-1
RELIGION / Christian Theology / Apologetics

Published by BMH books, Winona Lake, IN 46590
www.bmhbooks.com

Unless otherwise noted, Scripture verses are from the *New International Version*, copyright ©1973, 1978, 1984 by International Bible Society. Used by permission of Zondervan. All rights reserved.

Printed in the United States of America

Table of Contents

Introduction 1

Part I - My Story: God's Plan for My Life

Chapters 1-4, Summary 5

Part II - His Story: God's Plan for Humanity

Chapter 5, Thomas 11
Chapter 6, Moses 13
Chapter 7, Paul 16
Chapter 8, John 18

Part III - Your Story: God's Plan for Your Life

Chapter 9, Prayer 23
Chapter 10, Trust 25
Chapter 11, All Nations –All People 28
Chapter 12, Fear No Evil 30
Concluding Considerations 32

Introduction

This study guide is intended to be used as a supplement to *God of Hope*. It can be used for individual study, in a small group, or in an informal class situation. It is not intended to be a study in theology, politics, or psychology. Rather, its aim is to assist the reader to consider carefully the practical application of the stories outlined in the book.

The content of the book is presented in three parts. In the first section the author relates his own experience in discovering God's plan for his life. Though highly successful in business, he had to rediscover his faith in God, finally realizing that only through trusting God could he experience genuine hope.

Part II is God's story, His plan for humanity. Through the narratives of four biblical characters, the progressive revelation of God is explained. The frailties and failures of mankind are contrasted in the experiences related by the narrators with the outworking of the mysterious plan of God's grace that is the basis for the hope that humanity is continually seeking.

In Part III, "Your Story: God's Plan for Your Life," the author emphasizes the importance of prayer, trusting in the Bible, becoming a part of a community of believers, and the way to overcome fear. Early in life most people question "Why am I here? What is my purpose in life? What is the meaning of life?" Everyone at some time wonders about the spiritual side of life. Is there a God? If so, how can I know Him? Does He care about me and my life?

Each one must make an individual decision about a relationship with God and how one will relate to Him. Discussing the questions in this study guide will help you find answers to these questions and determine how you will respond to God.

Approach each chapter in the book with an open mind, seeking to learn, willing to respond to the truth you discover. Do not hesitate to express your doubts and raise your questions. Although faith inherently believes in what one cannot see and is often intangible, it is not irrational. One does not have to "turn off" the brain when approaching questions of spirituality and faith. Ask God for clear thinking and expect to experience growth and stimulation as you read and question.

God is incomprehensible yet knowable. Limited by our finite mind, we cannot fully understand God, but God has revealed Himself so we can know Him. The author has written *God of Hope* to stimulate the reader to consider carefully this question: *What do you believe? If you don't believe in God, what do you believe? Where will you find purpose for your life and hope for the future?*

Part I

MY STORY: GOD'S PLAN FOR MY LIFE

Chapters 1–4
Summary

Chapter 1: Playing Chess with God

The son of a Presbyterian pastor, the author drifted into non-belief, questioning how an intelligent person could believe in God. It seemed like a myth at that point in his life.

Finding himself with nothing else to do on one occasion, he picked up a Bible and read the Gospel of Mark from beginning to end. He says he "met a different God" at that time, and he "was stunned." At that moment he believed in his heart and "asked Jesus Christ into [his] life." He writes, "It was a defining moment in my life."

From that time on, his relationship with God helped to determine the course of his life and the decisions he had to make. Moved several times by the Chrysler Corporation, for whom he was a regional manager, he began to look elsewhere for work in a local retail dealership where he would not have to move again.

Through these experiences he became frustrated with the moves and the lack of a good job opportunity. He recalled that his father had taught him that God had a purpose for his life, but he felt as if he were a chess piece being moved about on the board of life.

Chapter 2: Lost in Detroit

Chrysler was going through financial difficulties and eventually received government loan guarantees and gained new leadership with Lee Iacocca. The author became more and more dissatisfied with his working conditions and continued to seek employment elsewhere. Pressures at home were building also, and it all came to an explosive incident on his way back to his hotel in Detroit one evening.

So severe was the author's frustration, that he lost his temper to the point of cursing God. But, in the midst of that emotional breakdown, he suddenly found peace and "felt that there was hope." Almost miraculously, after having been "lost in Detroit," he found himself at his destination right on schedule.

Chapter 3: Home at Last

In spite of many attempts to find work elsewhere (more than 600 résumés sent out), the author continued working for Chrysler. Offered a significant promotion to the front office, he turned it down. His reason: "I have three priorities in my life: #1 is Jesus Christ; #2 is my family; and #3 is Chrysler. I believe if I take this job, it will be changing my #1 and #2 priorities, and I just can't do that."

Finally, the author set a deadline. If he didn't receive a job offer in 60 days, he would stay with Chrysler. On the 59th day, Toyota offered him a job, and one month later he was working for Toyota in California. Immediately he noted the difference in the atmosphere and conduct of the office meetings. As a result he felt "Home at Last."

Chapter 4: An Answer to Prayer?

Thirty years later, enjoying a highly successful career with Toyota, the author was challenged by a Christian speaker who spoke about business leaders making a difference in the world. Hearing that challenge reminded him of a childhood promise he had made long ago to God: "Someday, I will write about the encounter between the unbelieving Thomas and Jesus, and I will do it right." Although he had had success in business writing, his many attempts at writing for publication had been rejected. He had asked God many times to allow him to be a speaker and author. But the answer always seemed to be, "No thank you." Until now.

His childhood promise came to mind when he saw a highway sign that showed the population of Los Angeles, at that time, to be 3,772,000. He realized that out of all those people in L.A. there was certainly someone better than he to share the gospel. He thought of excuses why he couldn't be the one to do it and asked, "Why me?" Then he seemed to hear an inner voice saying, "Because you can." So, his longtime prayer was finally answered.

God of Hope began then and has become a four-year project. The author has told his story in these four chapters, and he asks, "But what about 'God's story'?" Thus, he introduces the first of four narratives, finally telling the story of Thomas as he had planned so many years ago.

Discussion Questions

1. What most impressed you about the author's experience?
2. The author admits to cursing God. Is it okay to be upset with God?
3. The author says that after cursing God and weeping, he suddenly felt hope. How is that possible?
4. Was the author's move to a new job and ultimate successful employment there the work of God or just chance?
5. Have you ever felt that your job and life have become meaningless and unfulfilling? Describe how you felt and why.
6. Was there a sense of guilt? How did you handle it?

Think About This

- How do you answer these most basic questions of life? Does the author's experience give you any insight to these questions?
    - Who are you?
    - Where are you?
    - What are you doing here?
- Can one be a "borderline" Christian? What does that mean? Is that what the author was at the beginning of chapter 1?

- If you don't believe there is a God, what do you believe?
- Where does one find hope? Why is life worth living?
- What is the purpose and meaning of life?

Note

Part I is the story of a man who re-found his faith and discovered hope. He argues that if there is no God, there is no hope; life is purposeless and meaningless. In Part II you will discover where hope is to be found.

Part II

GOD'S STORY: GOD'S PLAN FOR HUMANITY

Chapter 5: Thomas
Listen to Your Heart

Summary

Thomas says he came to share his story so we could know the depth of God's love for us. Thomas was a Jew, an Israelite, and in his day Israel, politically, was under the harsh rule of Rome. Religiously, the people were under the direction of leaders who controlled them with countless rules but were in constant disagreement among themselves. Thus, the needs of the people were ignored.

Thomas confessed that he hated the Romans, was bitter toward the political rulers, and feared the religious leaders. Like most religious people of his day, he thought he could earn God's blessing by strict obedience to the law of Moses.

God had not spoken to His people through prophets for more than 400 years before John the Baptist came on the scene, promising that the long-awaited Messiah was coming. When the prophet Jesus came, Thomas, like many others, was drawn to Him, and he became one of His intimate 12 disciples, traveling and serving with Him for more than two years.

Despite Jesus' ministry of teaching and healing—even raising the dead on occasion—the religious leaders hated Him, were jealous of His popularity, and plotted to kill Him. They succeeded and Jesus was crucified by Rome at the insistence of the Jewish religious leaders who accused Him of blasphemy against God. His disciples fled in terror.

Just as He had promised, Jesus was raised from the dead. He appeared to His disciples on an occasion when Thomas was absent. Thomas could not believe the report of his companions, that they had actually seen Jesus; he demanded proof to satisfy his doubts. After all, how could the promised Messiah die in the first place? And further, having seen Him die, how could he believe that Jesus was now alive?

In one of the most amazing stories in the Bible, Jesus appeared to the disciples once again when Thomas was present. Immediately, the doubting disciple recognized Jesus as the risen Lord and fell to his knees in worship.

Discussion Questions

1. What would you have done at the crucifixion of Jesus if you had been in Thomas' sandals?
2. How did the death of Jesus confuse Thomas' expectations for the Messiah?
3. How do you explain Thomas' reluctance to believe that Jesus had arisen?
4. What do you think is a major purpose of Thomas' narration?

Think About This

- Is it wrong to question God?
- Dare we challenge God?
- Do you identify with Thomas' doubts? How would you have reacted at Jesus' appearance?

Note

Thomas related his story to encourage you to listen carefully to the next three witnesses.

Chapter 6: Moses
"I Am Has Sent Me"

Summary

Moses tells the story of the Israelites, God's chosen people, who were long-time slaves in Egypt. As the slave population increased, Pharaoh feared a potential uprising of the Hebrew people, so he took drastic measures to limit population growth by having all boy babies killed.

Moses was miraculously delivered as a baby and was raised in the home of Pharaoh's daughter. Thus, he became a prince of Egypt, highly educated and trained. After killing an Egyptian whom he saw beating a Hebrew slave, however, Moses fled into the wilderness where he lived for 40 years, surviving as a shepherd.

God made a spectacular appearance to Moses one day, speaking to him from a bush that was aflame but not consumed. He identified Himself as "I Am," a name previously unknown to the Israelites. God had chosen Moses to lead His people out of captivity into a Promised Land where they were to serve Him. Reluctant to obey, but finally assuming the responsibility and accompanied by his brother Aaron, Moses returned to Egypt and appealed to Pharaoh to let the Hebrew people leave Egypt to worship their God. Pharaoh was adamant and only increased the burden of the slave people.

God instructed Moses to threaten Pharaoh with a series of terrible plagues for his refusal to release His people. After the ninth plague—each struck at the foundational beliefs of the Egyptians and their false gods while the Israelites were protected from the plagues—Moses warned of a tenth calamity, the death of the Egyptians' firstborn children.

On the night of the promised deaths, God delivered His people, protected by the blood of sacrificial lambs sprinkled on their doorposts, and the multitude of thousands began their trek to the Promised Land. God provided miraculously for His people in their journey, delivering them again from Pharaoh when he attempted to recapture them at the Red Sea, and providing food and water throughout their desert journey.

God gave to Moses the Ten Commandments, which were to be the guidelines for His people perpetually, and, although they agreed to keep them, they were unfaithful. As they approached their new homeland, they balked when they saw how difficult it would be to take the land and conquer the inhabitants. For their lack of faith they were condemned to die in the desert and only two of the original cohort entered the land along with the multitude that had been born during the desert wanderings. Moses himself was not permitted to enter Canaan, but he led them to the border.

Discussion Questions

1. What is the significance of the name God used to identify Himself: "I Am"? (A Bible dictionary might be helpful.)

2. Why did Moses wear a veil after His meeting with God? Do we all wear veils? Why?

3. Read Hebrews 11:23-29 in the New Testament. What do you learn there about the faith of Moses?

Think About This

- Moses was a leader people followed. How was he able to demand obedience? Where did he get his authority?

- What picture of God do you get from the Ten Commandments?

- How do you stack up when it comes to obeying the Ten Commandments?

- Can anyone completely keep the Ten Commandments? What is the consequence of failure?

Note

God's plan is progressively revealed in the Bible. In the next chapter, Paul presents more detail about God's plan, which will give hope for those who trust in Him.

Chapter 7: Paul
God's Secret Plan

Summary

The story of the apostle Paul is a prime example of life transformation. Trained as a Jewish scholar, Saul—his birth name—was a religious zealot. Believing in strict adherence to the law of Moses, he valiantly fought against what he regarded as a new, false "religion," Christianity, sometimes referred to as "the Way."

So committed was Saul in his religious fervor that he gained the permission of the Jewish leaders to seek out and persecute Christians, whom he considered enemies of the Jewish faith. Saul was an eyewitness to, and abetted, the martyrdom of Stephen, an early leader of the Christian church.

The transformation of this religious zealot began on one of his journeys to persecute Christians. He had a miraculous encounter with one who identified Himself as Jesus Christ and appeared to Saul in a blinding light. Saul recognized Jesus as Lord and, though blinded temporarily by the vision, he began the spiritual journey that changed him from a zealot of Judaism to a zealous follower of Jesus. His name was changed to Paul, and he became the last of the apostles to have seen the risen Christ. Thus began an itinerant ministry which resulted in the establishment of churches all over the Middle East and the training of men to continue the ministry Paul launched.

In his narration Paul clearly lays out the basic tenets of Christianity: the helpless state of men who have rejected God, the sacrifice Jesus made on the cross to pay the penalty for men's turning away from God, the resurrection of Jesus as proof of the satisfactory payment, and the grace of God offered to all who will place their faith in the sacrifice of Jesus.

Paul was inspired by God to write many of the books of the New Testament of the Bible, letters to churches that continued the revelation of God's plan which had begun in the Old Testament. God had revealed His plan to Paul by the Holy Spirit. Paul recorded the great doctrines of Christianity and the practical application of those truths in his preaching and writing. The great apostle suffered greatly in his missionary career, but he remained faithful to the end.

Discussion Questions

1. Paul told of Gamaliel's warning (Acts 5:34-39) that if Peter were acting as a man, he would fail, but if his actions were of God, he could not be stopped, and the Jewish leaders would be enemies of God. Is that true? Was his warning fulfilled?
2. What makes Paul's preaching and writing credible?
3. How does Paul compare the evil of his day to the evil of today?
4. What is Paul's suggested remedy for today's evil?

Think About This

- How do you explain the change in Saul from a violent zealot to a compassionate servant?
- What can change a man from a life of violence and hatred to a life of love and sacrifice?
- What is God's secret plan?
- How do you explain the turmoil of the 21st century, the atrocities, inhuman treatment of fellow human beings, and genocide? What is the solution espoused by Paul?

Note

Paul's preaching is not a contradiction of the Old Testament but a continuing revelation of God's plan that fulfills the law of Moses and provides a way by God's grace to be restored to favor with God.

Chapter 8: John
A New Heaven – A New Earth

Summary

When the apostle John recorded the Revelation, the final book of the New Testament of the Bible, he was the last survivor of the 12 disciples. One of the three who were closest to Jesus—the others were Jesus' brother James and Peter—John had an amazing vision of Jesus, whose life, death, and resurrection he had witnessed personally.

In this vision John was instructed to record what he "[had] seen, what is now and what will take place later" (Rev. 1:19). His record includes a number of visions God gave him that present what today we might call "bad news and good news." Because of the evil in the world and mankind's general rejection of God, numerous judgments are to come upon the earth—frightening catastrophes that will destroy human and animal lives and even the Earth. These judgments are so great that survivors will despair of life itself. The events culminate with the ultimate destruction of the evil one, evil itself at the deepest level.

The good news is that John in his visions of heaven also saw his Lord, Jesus Christ, as the Lamb of God. It is Jesus who brings judgment upon the wicked world, but it is He, also, who has provided for men to be redeemed by faith in His work. So, the good news is for those who accept God's grace and find forgiveness through faith in Jesus. For them there will be a celebratory banquet in heaven and the experiencing of an unending life of joy, peace, and fulfillment in the presence of the Triune God.

Discussion Questions

1. How does John describe the one who spoke to him on the Isle of Patmos?

2. In his narration John says that many today "believe that mankind is on the leading edge of human development… [and that] the world is made up of good people…progressing to a better, fuller, more perfect end." How do you evaluate those comments? Is that the same world you see?

3. How do you answer John's questions: "Is there life after death? What is more difficult, to be born the first time or reborn the second?"

Think About This

- Remember that John was an eyewitness to the bloody, violent mistreatment and death of Jesus. How do you react to his testimony?

- Jesus had told His disciples of His impending death and ultimate resurrection, but they had difficulty in understanding what it all meant. After the resurrection, they did not immediately believe. Likewise, Jesus has told of His coming again, yet many today find it hard to believe it is going to happen. Why?

- Having heard the testimony of these biblical, historical characters, do you have any further insight to answer these basic questions?
    o Who are you?
    o Where are you?
    o What are you doing here?

Notes

- Jesus, as the Lamb of God, fulfills the Old Testament prophetic symbols of the blood sacrifices and the lambs' blood sprinkled on the doorposts in Egypt that provided for the Israelites being passed over when the angels of death and judgment struck the neighboring Egyptians.

- Do you believe John's testimony? He was an eyewitness of the life, death, and resurrection of Jesus. He recognized Him both in His appearance to him on Patmos and in his visions of heaven.

- The revealing of God's plan began with the promise in Genesis of a savior to come, continued through the giving of the law with its symbolic sacrifices, was made possible through the sacrifice of Jesus, is explained more fully in the New Testament, and will come to completion as foretold in the final book of the Bible.

- In Part III you will be challenged to consider what your part is to be in God's plan.

Part III

YOUR STORY: GOD'S PLAN FOR YOUR LIFE

Chapter 9
Prayer

Summary

The author and his family, along with other volunteers, regularly work with a mission agency to build homes for needy residents and churches in Mexico. This chapter tells the story of one such visit and the very difficult circumstances in which the team suffered, largely because of extreme weather conditions.

In the midst of the trials, the author overhears the prayer of a poor local resident. She seemed to be in distress, and he prayed that God would hear her and relieve her of the burden. In reality, he later discovered, she was praying, not for herself, but for the volunteer team.

The author notes that the old woman's prayer was answered; the team successfully completed its project in spite of the difficult conditions. Subsequent volunteer teams frequently recall that special mission trip and the value of sincere, humble prayer.

Discussion Questions

1. What are some lessons you think the author might have learned from the old Mexican woman's prayer?
2. Describe an experience when someone else's prayer affected you in a meaningful way.
3. Is prayer more than mere hoping? If so, how?

Think About This

- When you pray, do you feel you are in touch with God? Why or why not?

- What do you think about this statement: "The effectiveness of prayer depends upon the One to whom one prays rather than the pray-er"?

Notes

- "The real value of persistent prayer is not so much that we get what we want as that we become the person we should be" (Philip Yancey).

- Chapter 10 will emphasize the worthiness of the Bible as the conveyor of truth in which we can place our trust unreservedly.

Chapter 10
Trust

Summary

This chapter asserts the authenticity and reliability of the Bible, the revelation of God in which men can confidently trust. The Bible is set in contrast to other well-known ancient literature, such as the works of Plato and Homer's *Iliad*. There are very few extant copies of that literature, and those copies are dated more than 1,000 years after the original writing. Yet, scholars consider them to record accurately the authors' words.

In contrast the Bible is often scorned by the critics as being unreliable. Yet, there are hundreds of extant copies of portions of the Old Testament, some dated as early as 250 B.C. The *Dead Sea Scrolls*, for example, are considered to be 95 percent identical to manuscripts dated 1,000 years later. There are more than 5,000 manuscripts of the New Testament, and the oldest were written within 100 years of the events by eyewitnesses or people who knew the eyewitnesses. Those manuscripts have 99.5 percent accuracy.

Writers of other early literature (e.g. Josephus and Tacitus) also give testimony to many of the historical events recorded in the New Testament and in early church history.

The origin of the biblical text is discussed briefly in this chapter, particularly with reference to its inspiration, meaning that it was authored by God as He caused human writers to record His revelation. Thus, those portions of Scripture that deal with events yet future to their writing are accurate, because God cannot err or lie. The Bible's prophecies have either been fulfilled as promised or are yet to be so.

Chapter 10 concludes with the recitation of several passages from Paul's letter to the Romans, intended to summarize God's plan for people whom He wishes to redeem from their sin, restore to a right relationship with Him, and give the assurance of a certain hope for the future.

Discussion Questions

1. How does the author use ancient literary works to support his contention that the Bible is reliable? Why do you think so many still question the authenticity of the Bible?

2. What impact has the discovery of the *Dead Sea Scrolls* had regarding the authenticity of the Bible?

3. Why do you think the Bible is the most published book in the world and at the same time is the subject of the harshest criticism from so many?

4. Read 2 Timothy 3:16 and 1 Peter 1:20-21 in the New Testament. What do these verses tell us about the Scriptures? What does *inspiration* ("God-breathed") suggest to you? What does Peter say about the ultimate origin of the Scriptures? What (or who) inspired the prophets to write? In light of such testimony, what are the reasons some reject the Bible as God's Word?

Think About This

- How do you respond to Paul's teaching in the Bible passages quoted in this chapter? Have those texts stimulated you to think more seriously about God's plan for you?

- What does *trust* mean? Is there any reason that you would refuse to accept God's Word and trust Jesus for your salvation and hope?

- Some people do believe in God and some don't and actually turn away and follow evil, but the majority of people do neither and go their own selfish ways. In which group are you?

Notes

- The Bible was given to reveal God and to enable people to do God's work in His world.

- Everyone trusts in certain realities every day, many of which they do not necessarily understand. Can one really trust in something he or she cannot see? Check out Jesus' words to Thomas in John 20:29.

- Although we may not be able to understand all about God, still we can know Him.

Chapter 11
All Nations—All Peoples

Summary

The church is defined here as "the community of believers," an appropriate description of those who hold in common a firm trust in Jesus Christ as Savior and Lord. Jesus promised He would build His church and nothing could overcome it (Matthew 16:18).

God promised Abraham in the first book of the Bible that He would bless all nations and people through him. The New Testament makes it clear that it's not the physical descendants of Abraham that He spoke of, but his spiritual descendants—those, who like him, put their complete faith in God.

Relating the dramatic experience of Joni Eareckson Tada, both a heart-wrenching and heart-warming story, the author illustrates one of the purposes of the church: protection from the shattering personal tragedies of life through the family of believers. God's support is often given through the help and assistance of one's spiritual family, the local community of believers. Joni testifies, "My church made a huge difference in my family's life as they demonstrated the love of God in practical ways."

Chapter 11 is an encouragement to affiliate with the church, the local community of believers, for the mutual benefit of each member and to the glory of God as He works through the church.

Discussion Questions

1. What did William Wilberforce, Dietrich Bonhoeffer, and Martin Luther King, Jr. have in common?

2. According to the author, what are the purposes of the church? Have you seen churches that demonstrate those purposes well?

3. What is to be learned from the tragic experience of Joni Eareckson Tada? How would you respond if you were to have a similar experience? Where would you look for help and hope?

Think About This

- How do you see the church in its helping role?

- Why do bad things happen to good people? What do you think would be God's answer?

Notes

- A fully committed follower of Jesus is not a loner; he or she associates with a community of believers.

- Christ-followers strive to support fellow believers and to share their faith with those who are not yet followers.

- There's more to being a Christ-follower than just trusting Him for salvation. You don't ever stop learning and growing—another reason for being involved with a community of believers.

Chapter 12
Fear No Evil

Summary

It's an old but dramatic story. The persecution of the church began in its very earliest years. Remember the zealous hatred of Saul of Tarsus and his persecution of followers of "the Way"? After his conversion, Paul himself was the subject of persecution, and he suffered multiple injuries and injustices because of his faith and testimony for Jesus.

The Roman rulers in the early Christian era seemed to delight in encouraging the violent "sports" of the people that culminated in the almost frivolous torture of Christians. This was exemplified in the Colosseum spectacles and the frequent crucifixion of believers. As in our own day, cruelty seems to feed on itself, and bloodthirsty crowds seem only to become more intense in their demand for violence.

Telemachus, a monk from Asia, was in the Colosseum on one occasion and witnessed the horrifying bloodshed. Eventually, he strode into the arena, shouting, "In the name of Christ, stop!" At the moment his efforts were futile, for he himself was beaten by the gladiators and stoned by the crowd. He sacrificed his life to protest the killing. Ultimately, however, the emperor declared an end to the gladiator combats. So, Telemachus' courageous stand was successful after all.

The challenge of chapter 12 is for the readers to follow in the path pursued by a host of men and women, who stepped out to do right without fear of evil. Psalm 23, perhaps the most familiar passage in the Bible, is quoted as an encouragement and challenge to fight evil in life wherever it is exposed. Then, the follower of Jesus will play his or her role in God's plan to establish a New Heaven and a New Earth.

Discussion Questions

1. Was the attempt of Telemachus to stop the killing of gladiators in the Roman Colosseum in vain?

2. Where would you find the kind of faith that would give you the courage to take a stand like Telemachus took?

3. What is the lesson to be learned from Bishop Wright's story about the stonemason and his work on the great cathedral? Does it have any application for you today?

4. Where does the author suggest that hope is to be found? Do you have that kind of hope (certain expectation)?

Think About This

- Hope is not an emotion but a confident assurance in anticipation of a fulfilled promise. Is that different from your hope for the future? If so, how?

- Do you know where to find your place in God's plan?

Notes

- Consider the source of hope that will enable you to move ahead without fear.

- Choice is one of the very few elements in life that you can control. What are the critical choices each of us must make in light of God's revelation? Have you made the choice to trust God?

- Of all the countless choices you make in a lifetime, the most important choice in life is what you will do with Jesus Christ. Do you acknowledge Him as the Son of God, as He claimed to be?

Concluding Considerations

1. The author's experience (chapters 1-4) demonstrates the futility of finding one's own way and the necessity of faith in One who is above earthly life's circumstances and offers assurance and hope in following Him. Have you found hope in the midst of life's ever-changing conditions and values? The author suggests that such hope cannot be found in the things of this life but in the Author of life, who gave His life to provide eternal life to those who believe in Him.

2. Many today are like Jesus' disciples who found it difficult at first to believe in the resurrection. The disciple Thomas discovered that faith must rise above the apparent realities of life and find hope in the reality of trust in the risen Jesus. He ultimately believed because He saw the risen Jesus, although he did not touch and feel as he had demanded. Jesus commended his belief but stated, "Blessed are those who have not seen and yet have believed" (John 20:29). Do you wish to believe in Jesus and His work to save you?

3. Moses was the lawgiver; he presented God's Ten Commandments. Israel demonstrated, however (as we all have), that men cannot keep God's law completely. His own disobedience kept him from entering the Promised Land, and only two (Joshua and Caleb) of the original cohort that left Egypt entered the land. If we cannot keep the law satisfactorily, what hope is there for us? Moses promised that God would "raise up a prophet like me" (Deuteronomy 18:15), a clear reference to Israel's Messiah, Jesus Christ. The Bible also clearly contrasts the difference between

the law given by Moses and grace and truth which came through Jesus (John 1:17). Jesus fulfilled the law, lived it perfectly, and satisfied the just demands of God by paying the penalty for all law-breakers.

4. Paul is an example of a completely transformed life. His testimony illustrates the transforming power of God's love when one encounters God through faith in Jesus Christ. At first, he was a zealous follower of God and keeper of the law, but he was ignorant of its true significance. After his miraculous conversion, he was an even more zealous follower of God, now recognizing Jesus as his Messiah, Savior, and Lord. Coming to a studied understanding of the Old Testament, he was the author of letters to early churches, explaining the theological basis for Christianity and giving instructions for the conduct of the Church of which Jesus is the head. The Book of Romans, in particular, explains God's great plan for the salvation of men and women. Read it carefully with an open mind, ready to receive its truth and acknowledge the God who is revealed there.

5. The apostle John was the last living disciple of Jesus when the Revelation was given to him. Through unusual visions and unearthly experiences, he was instructed to write about things that had been, things that were, and things that were to come (Revelation 1:19). If one understands nothing else from this highly-symbolic writing, the reader must at least acknowledge the severity of judgments to come upon the earth and mankind. Chapter 20 speaks of a judgment at a "great white throne" (vv. 11-15), which seems to be a final condemnation of all who have rejected Jesus, whose names are "not found written in the book of life" (v. 15). Consider this important question: Is your name written in the book of life? If not, do you know how to have it inscribed there?

6. What do you understand prayer to be? Is it merely wishful thinking, addressing an unknown (perhaps unknowable) greater being? Is it only a self-initiated, mind-clearing exercise? Or is it,

in reality, a conversation with a sovereign but personal, loving God, a two-way conversation that seeks to know God and effect change? Remember this statement: "There is only one fatal mistake you can make about prayer and that is to stop praying and not begin again." But that prayer must be addressed to the one true God as revealed in the Bible and in Jesus Christ.

7. Having learned about the reliability, authenticity, and integrity of the Bible, how has it changed your life? Have you started reading it regularly? It is in His Word that we learn of God's plan and find our place in that plan.

8. If you have come to know God personally through a faith relationship with Jesus, have you begun to associate with a community of believers, a local church? Although you can worship God alone, there is so much to be gained by corporate worship: personal and group encouragement, magnified praise of God, growth through common fellowship in worship. Also, it's the church's responsibility to tell the world about God, and that is most effectively accomplished through the cooperative effort of believers. Are you involved in the local community's outreach ministries? The author has stated, "The church also exists ... [to offer] believers protection from the shattering personal tragedies of life, and through fellow believers in the church, [God] provides a maximum of support to meet these tragedies." Perhaps you're not going through a time of stress right now, but when you do face situations of struggle, where will you turn if you don't have a strong relationship with a church? Look around you in the community of believers. Is there another Joni Eareckson Tada you could be helping? There very well may be someone who needs your encouragement today. How are you preparing to help in those situations?

9. You'll not likely ever witness a Colosseum where gladiators are fighting to kill, where Christians are beset by lions. On the other hand, it is reported that there are more Christian martyrs worldwide today than at any other time in history. Perhaps

you're living close to such atrocities. Maybe you're even a victim, deprived of human rights because of your faith in Jesus. Are you trusting in your own strength, or in the power of governments or world opinion to deliver you? Or, are you learning to trust in God alone who promises that you can "fear no evil" because He is with you? If you're not a victim but are aware of Christians suffering for His name's sake, what can you do to help? Can you do something other than pray? Plan for ways you can help those suffering nearby or far away.

10. After having read *God of Hope*, can you say with the author, "As for me and my house, we choose hope—the God of Hope"? If not and you have questions, please check the God of Hope website for help. If you have trusted Jesus, make every effort to pursue these three objectives: 1) make public your profession of faith in Jesus as your savior; 2) find and join a community of believers (a local church) where God's Word is believed fully and taught faithfully; and 3) develop a life strategy that includes specific plans for Bible reading and study, prayer, encouragement for fellow believers, and outreach activities to share the gospel with those who've not yet come to belief in Christ.

Final Thoughts

- Consider the reason the apostle John gives for writing his Gospel: "These are written that you may believe that Jesus is the Christ, the Son of God, and that by believing you may have life in his name" (John 20:31).

- God "left" earth's scene because of evil, but He came back in Jesus to overcome evil and will come back once again to forever destroy evil and establish an everlasting kingdom. Some in earlier times had difficulty believing that the Messiah would come. Like them, many today have disregarded the teaching of the Second Coming of Christ and are unable to believe it will happen. But that is the Christian's hope: "while we wait for the blessed hope—the glorious appearing of our great God and Savior, Jesus Christ" (Titus 2:13).

- The single most important question in life is "What do you think of Jesus?" Is He God, as He claimed to be?

- Consider this critical statement posed by C. S. Lewis: "A man who was merely a man and said the sort of things Jesus said would not be a great moral teacher. He would either be a lunatic—on the level with the man who says he is a poached egg—or else he would be the Devil of Hell. You must make a choice. Either this man was, and is, the Son of God, or else a madman or something worse." [1]

- Understanding Jesus' claims and the reason for His life and sacrifice should help you answer these most basic questions:
    - Who are you?
    - Where are you?
    - What are you doing here?

- To believe or not to believe is a choice. You may choose to believe or not to believe. But realize that not making a choice is a decision, and it has consequences.

- If you don't believe there is a God, where will you find purpose for your life and hope for the future?

---

[1] C.S. Lewis, *Mere Christianity* (New York, HarperCollins Publishers, 1952), pp. 55-56.

GOD OF HOPE

Look for these companion products to the book!

Study and discussion guide
For use by individuals, small groups, or classes at church or school.

Audio and Video Products

Look for them at
www.godofhope.net